The Widow and the Prophet

CW00530019

Copyright © 2022 by Miiko Shaffier
All rights reserved. No part of this book may be reproduced in any manner whatsoever without prior written permission from the author, except in the case of brief quotations in reviews for inclusion in a magazine, newspaper or broadcast.

BY MIIKO SHAFFIER
co-written by Chana Grosser

Illustrated by: Dmitry Gitelman (diemgi.com)
Layout & Design by: Ken Parker (visual-variables.com)

Published by:
Shefer Publishing
www.SheferPublishing.com

For permissions, comments and ordering information write:
Miiko@LearnHebrew.tv

ISBN 978-0-9978675-6-5

THE
WIDOW
AND THE PROPHET

an **EASY EEVREET STORY**

BY MIIKO SHAFFIER

SHEFER
PUBLISHING

Based on *2 Kings*, *Chapter 4*, *verses 4-10*.
Read this story like any English story book.
When you get to a Hebrew word, do your best
to sound it out and guess the meaning. You can
check the pronunciation and meaning in the back
of the book.

HAVE FUN!

KNOCK. KNOCK.
The אִשָּׁה inside could hear the voice loud and clear.

5

"Your husband has died, I know that! But he has left many debts. He owes me money! If you can't pay the debts, I want your two children. They will be my עֲבָדִים. I will be back for either money or עֲבָדִים."

The אִשָּׁה did exactly what the prophet ehLeeYSHah' had told her. She went to her שְׁכֵנִים and borrowed many כֵּלִים jars and רֵיקִים.

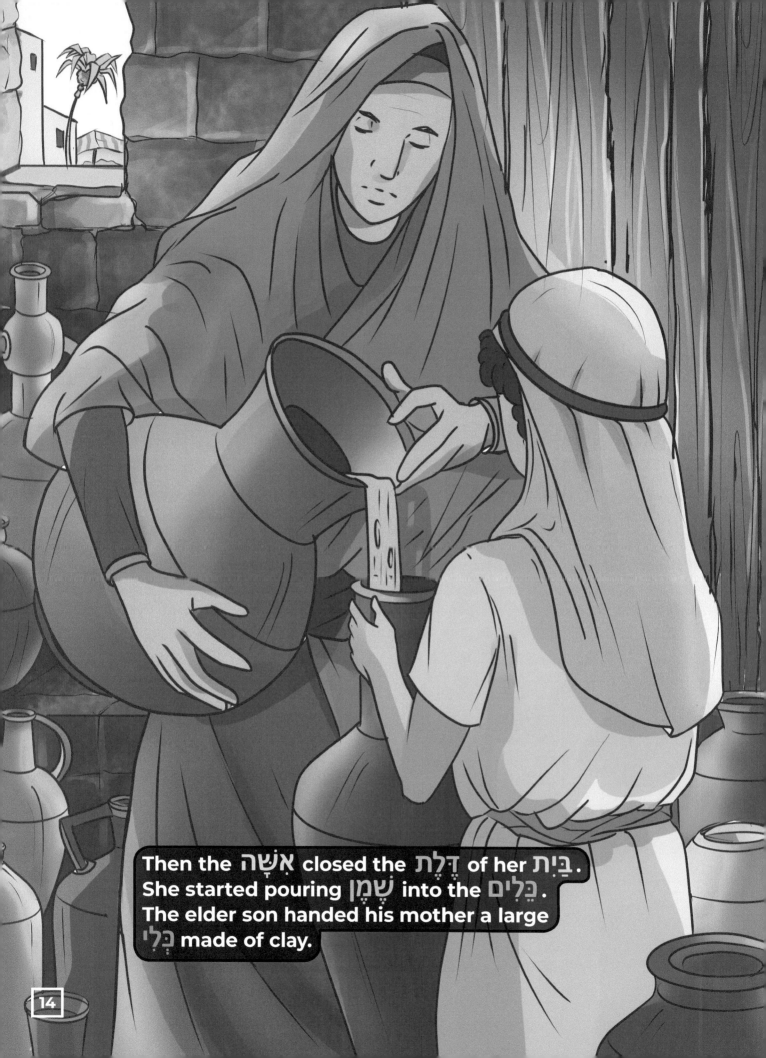

Then the אִשָּׁה closed the דֶּלֶת of her בַּיִת.
She started pouring שֶׁמֶן into the כֵּלִים.
The elder son handed his mother a large
כְּלִי made of clay.

The אִשָׁה poured the שֶׁמֶן, and the שֶׁמֶן dripped. The אִשָׁה poured the שֶׁמֶן, and the שֶׁמֶן kept flowing!

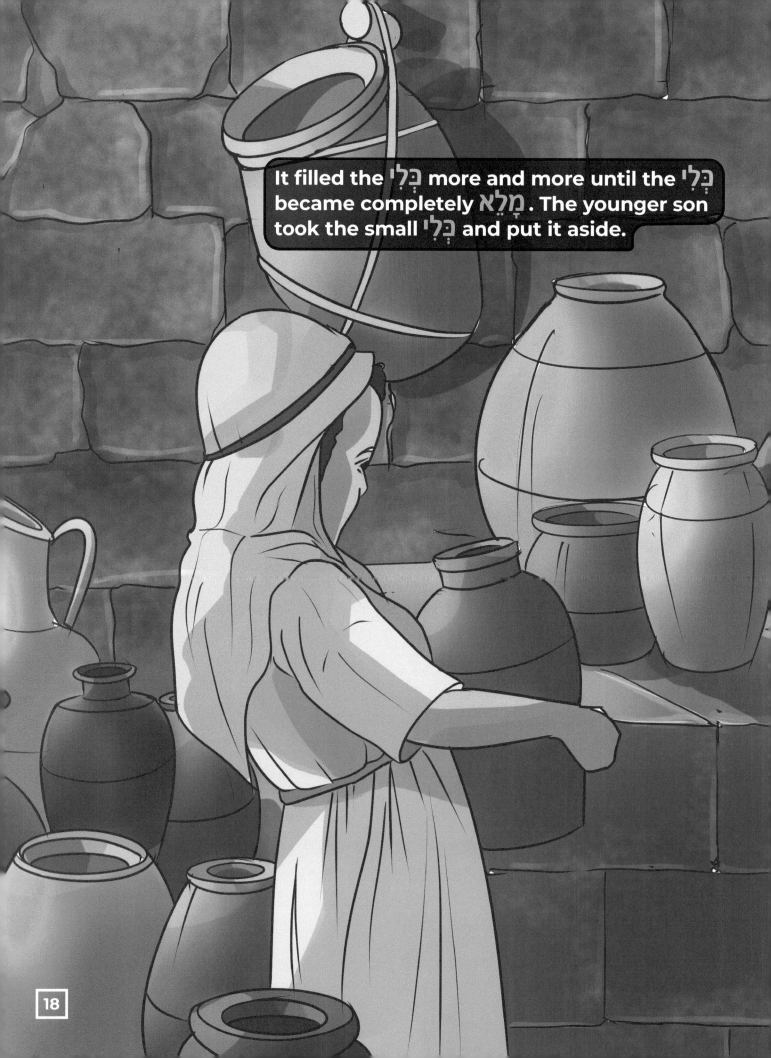

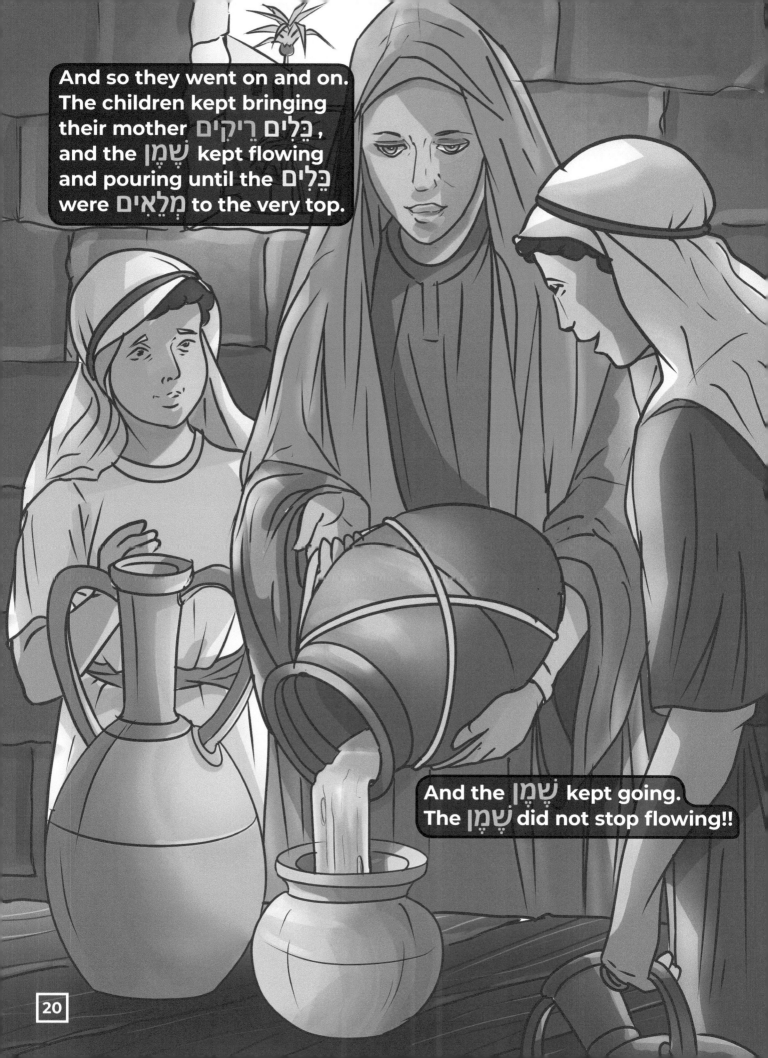

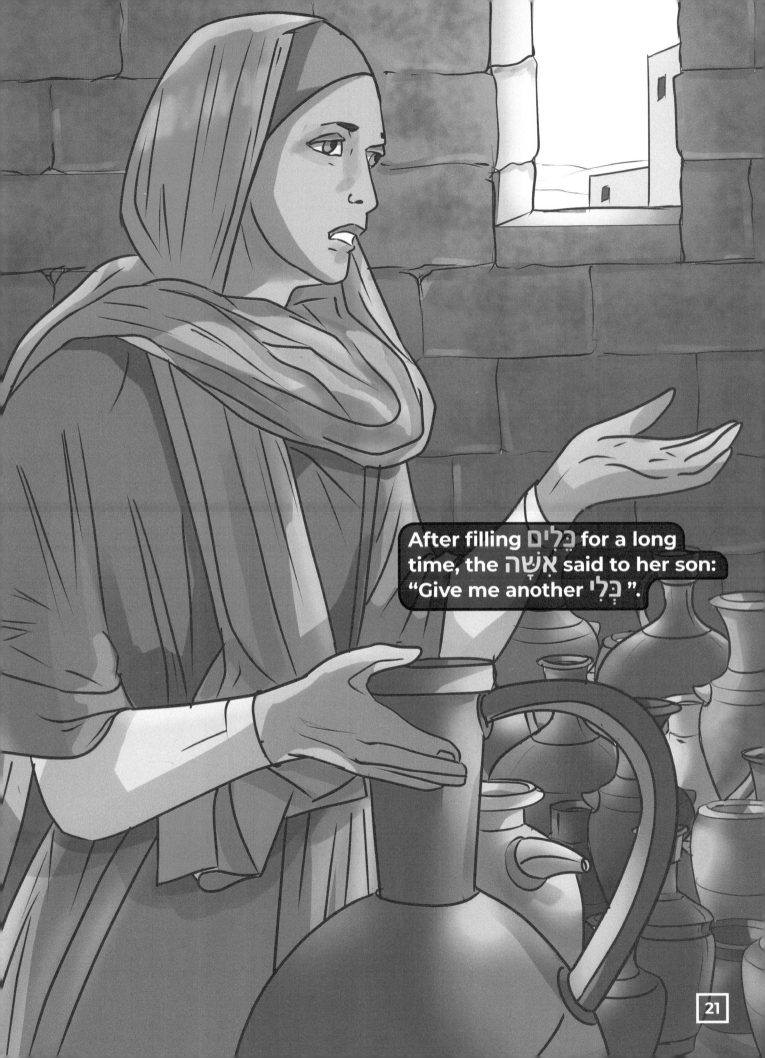

After filling כֵּלִים for a long time, the אִשָּׁה said to her son: "Give me another כְּלִי".

There were no כֵּלִים רֵיקִים in the back.
There were no כֵּלִים רֵיקִים in the front.
There were no כֵּלִים רֵיקִים left at all.

So the son said to his mother: "There are no more כֵּלִים רֵיקִים". And at that moment, the שֶׁמֶן stopped flowing.

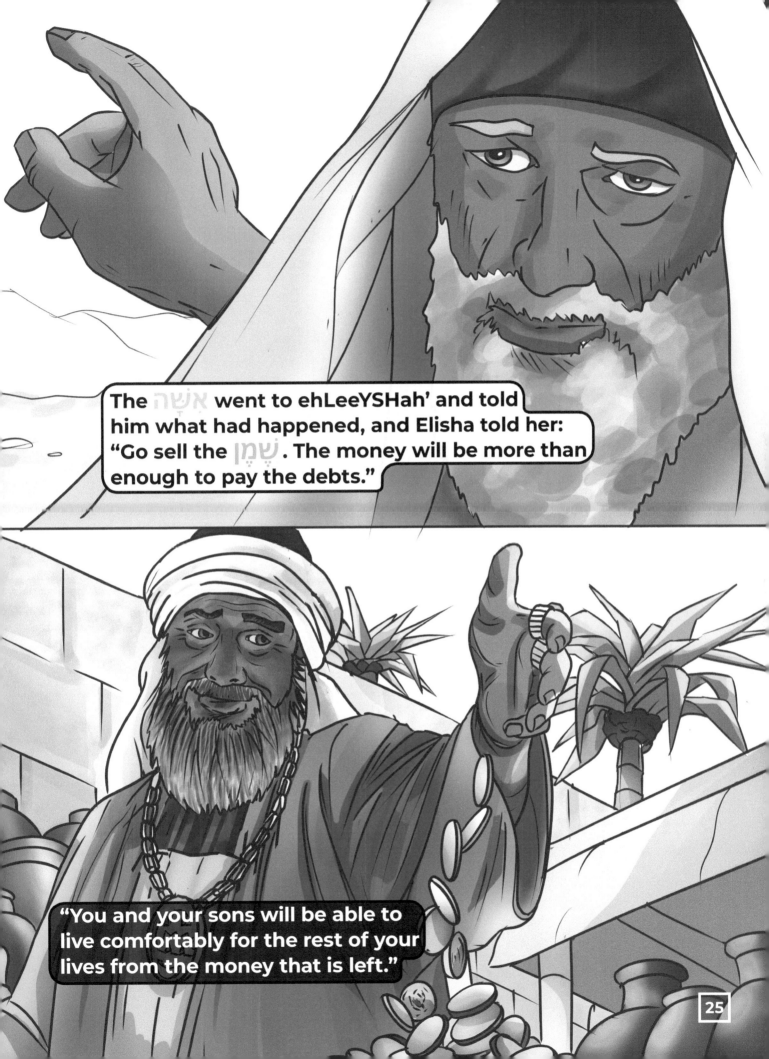

The אִשָּׁה went to ehLeeYSHah' and told him what had happened, and Elisha told her: "Go sell the שֶׁמֶן. The money will be more than enough to pay the debts."

"You and your sons will be able to live comfortably for the rest of your lives from the money that is left."

Here are the Hebrew words from this Easy Eevreet story:

 אִשָּׁה
'eeYSHahH - **WOMAN** | p. 5,8,11,13, 14,15,17,21,25

 עֲבָדִים
'ahVahDeeYM - **SLAVES** | p. 6,8

If it's only one slave the word is:

עֶבֶד 'ehVehD - **SLAVE**

עוֹבֵד 'ohVehD - **WORKER OR EMPLOYEE**

עֲבוֹדָה 'ahVohDahH - **WORK**

 נָבִיא
NahVeeY' - **PROPHET** | p. 8,9

 לָקַחַת
LahKahCHahT - **TO TAKE** | p. 8

The word קַח means take. When you add the letter ל to the beginning of a word it's like adding the word 'to'.

 בַּיִת
BahYeeT - **HOUSE** | p. 10,14

שֶׁמֶן
SHehMehN - **OIL** | p. 11,12,14,15,16, 17,19,20,24,25

 שְׁכֵנִים SH-CHehNeeYM - **NEIGHBORS** | p. 12,13

If it's only one neighbor the word is:

שָׁכֵן SHahCHehN - **NEIGHBOR**

כֵּלִים KehLeeYM - **VESSELS** | p. 12,13,14,16, 20,21,23,24

If it's only one vessel use the word:

כְּלִי K-LeeY - **VESSEL** | p. 12,14,16,18,21

רֵיקִים RehYKeeYM - **EMPTY** (plural) | p. 12,13,20, 23,24

In Hebrew the words in a sentence are in a different order than how we speak in English. In English we say "empty vessels" but in Hebrew it would be "vessels empty." In Hebrew, the description word (the adjective) also needs to be plural.

EMPTY VESSELS

כֵּלִים רֵיקִים - KehLeeYM (vessels) RehYKeeYM (empty)

If you want to describe only one thing as being empty use this word:

רֵיק RehYK - **EMPTY**

כְּלִי רֵיק K-LeeY (vessel) RehYK (empty) - **EMPTY VESSEL**

דֶּלֶת | DehLehT - **DOOR** | p. 12,14

מָלֵא | MahLeh' - **FULL** | p. 12,16,18,20

מְלָאִים | M-Leh'eeYM - **FULL** (plural) | p. 20

Again we see how Hebrew sentences are written in a different order than English sentences are. In English we say "full vessel" but in Hebrew it would be "vessel full." We also see how the description word (the adjective) must be plural.

כְּלִי מָלֵא K-LeeY (vessel) MahLe' (full) - **FULL VESSEL**

FULL VESSELS
כֵּלִים מְלָאִים KehLeeYM (vessels) M-Leh'eeYM (full)

Now you know some pretty awesome Hebrew words. You can use your Hebrew words around the house or with friends. It'll be fun to close the דֶּלֶת or ask for a מָלֵא cup of water. Just try to stay away from convincing your friend to be your עֶבֶד.

Hi!

My name is **Miiko**. I live in Be'er Sheva, Israel. My husband Aaron and I have nine kids: Menucha, Mendel, Dovi, Yisroel, Freida, Devora, Fitche, Geula, and Azaria.

I teach Hebrew reading with a fun little book called *Learn to Read Hebrew in 6 Weeks!*

My second book *The Hebrew Workbook* teaches readers to write in Hebrew.

The Widow and The Prophet is part of a series of storybooks that teach Hebrew vocabulary to kids.

I'm so pleased to be a part of your Hebrew journey. If you have any questions or want to say hi please send me an email! **Miiko@LearnHebrew.tv**

To the Parents

This book is designed to teach Hebrew vocabulary to people who already know how to read the Hebrew alphabet. While reading this Bible story in English you'll come across Hebrew words embedded in the text. Sound out the words and try to guess their meaning from the context. Check the key in the back of the book to see if you were right.

I've chosen to transliterate the names of the biblical characters mentioned in this story so that you'll learn the authentic Hebrew pronunciation of these biblical names.

Transliteration

The Widow and The Prophet uses the same system of transliteration as my first book *Learn to Read Hebrew in 6 Weeks!*

I came up with a unique transliteration system. It's designed to have the reader pronouncing the Hebrew words accurately without ever having heard a Hebrew speaker pronounce those words.

Here's a breakdown of the system:

Each consonant is represented as a capital letter and each vowel by small letters.

The silent letters 'ahLehF (א) and 'ahYeeN (ע) are represented by an apostrophe (')

The silent vowel 'Sh-Vah' (:) is represented as a hyphen (-).

An important exception to make note of:
The CH does not represent the ch sound like in *chair* or *chest*. In fact, Hebrew doesn't have the ch sound like *chair* or *chest* at all.

The CH represents the letters CHehT(ח) and CHahF(כ) and Final ChahF(ך.) These letters make a sound not found in the English language. It's a chokey sound that almost sounds like a kitten purring but much harsher. Think about the name of the composer Bach. From what my Spanish speaking students tell me, it's the same sound as the guttural J in Spanish.

Let's look at the first word in the Hebrew Scripture as an example of how my system works:

בְּרֵאשִׁית

I transliterate it:
B-Reh'SHeeYT

Others may transliterate Bereshit or Bresheet but then you wouldn't know if the vowels are long or short.

If you learned to read Hebrew using my other book, you are already well familiar with this system. But in case you learned to read Hebrew elsewhere, here's a key to make sure it's clear.

א	ב	ב	ג	ד	ה	ו
'	B	V	G	D	H	V

ז	ח	ט	י	כּ	כ	ך
Z	CH	T	Y	K	CH	CH

ל	מ	ם	נ	ן	ס	ע
L	M	M	N	N	S	'

פּ	פ	ף	צ	ץ	ק	ר
P	F	F	TZ	TZ	K	R

שׁ	ת	ת
SH	T	T

דָ	וּ	וֹ	וּ	ֵ	ִ	ְ
ah	eh	oo	oh	ee	-

LEARN TO READ AND WRITE HEBREW WITH MY FUN AND EASY SYSTEM!

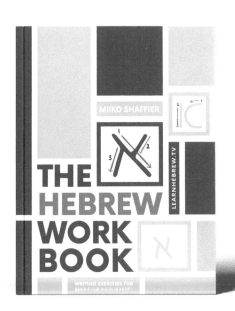

#1 BESTSELLERS
IN HEBREW LANGUAGE INSTRUCTION

- ▸ FUN MEMORY TRICKS
- ▸ 12 SIMPLE LESSONS
- ▸ PACED TO FINISH IN 6 WEEKS
- ▸ LEARN TO READ THE HEBREW BIBLE
- ▸ GREAT FOR ADULTS OR CHILDREN ALIKE
- ▸ CHARMING ILLUSTRATIONS TO MAKE LEARNING HEBREW A PLEASURE

MORE DETAILS AT LEARNHEBREW.TV
AVAILABLE AT AMAZON

Milton Keynes UK
Ingram Content Group UK Ltd.
UKHW051432100324
439268UK00002B/18